STUDEBAKER
1946 THROUGH 1958
PHOTO ARCHIVE

STUDEBAKER
1946 THROUGH 1958
PHOTO ARCHIVE

Edited with introduction by
Howard L. Applegate

Iconografix
Photo Archive Series

Iconografix
PO Box 18433
Minneapolis, Minnesota 55418 USA

Library of Congress Card Number 94-79320

ISBN 1-882256-25-5

95 96 97 98 99 00 5 4 3 2 1

Cover and book design by Lou Gordon, Osceola, Wisconsin

Printed in the United States of America

Book trade distribution by Voyageur Press, Inc. (800) 888-9653

PREFACE

The histories of machines and mechanical gadgets are contained in the books, journals, correspondence and personal papers stored in libraries and archives throughout the world. Written in tens of languages, covering thousands of subjects, the stories are recorded in millions of words.

Words are powerful. Yet, the impact of a single image, a photograph or an illustration, often relates more than dozens of pages of text. Fortunately, many of the libraries and archives that house the words also preserve the images.

In the *Photo Archive Series*, Iconografix reproduces photographs and illustrations selected from public and private collections. The images are chosen to tell a story—to capture the character of their subject. Reproduced as found, they are accompanied by the captions made available by the archive.

The Iconografix *Photo Archive Series* is dedicated to young and old alike, the enthusiast, the collector and anyone who, like us, is fascinated by "things" mechanical.

1946 Skyway Champion four-door six-passenger cruising sedan.

INTRODUCTION

The history of Studebaker began in 1852 when two brothers, Henry and Clem opened an Indiana blacksmith shop where they specialized in the manufacture of horse drawn farm wagons. In a few years, they were joined by three other brothers, John Mohler, Jacob, and Peter. Soon the family firm evolved into the Studebaker Brothers Manufacturing Company. The company's publicity claimed that the brothers were the world's largest maker of horse drawn vehicles. The brothers were slow to recognize the fact that the motor vehicle would permanently replace all horse drawn equipment, so they entered the automotive market cautiously and late. Starting in 1902, they made and sold small electric cars; beginning in 1904 they sold cars essentially made to their specifications by the Garford company of Ohio. The brothers established the Studebaker Corporation in 1910, after they acquired the E-M-F Company of Detroit. Thereafter, the Studebakers themselves manufactured all their vehicular products.

The 1920's were the Golden Age of the Studebaker Corporation. Not only was it recognized as a premiere manufacturer of quality cars and trucks, but the company made money and lots of it during the early and middle Twenties. Albert R. Erskine, who had become corporate president in 1915, did not expect the Great Depression that began in 1929 to be of long duration, so he continued to pay out vast sums of company money in the form of dividends, even when the firm began to show annual deficits. Erskine's financial follies caused him to commit suicide. In the 1930's, therefore, Studebaker had its ups and downs. The company went into receivership in 1933 and probably would have closed except for the visionary efforts of President Paul Hoffman including the famous Champion line of cars introduced in 1939. For a company that made few profits in the 1930's and had many years with losses, the corporate financial position was greatly enhanced with profits during the war years from cost plus defense contracts. Studebaker was a quality producer of many military products, not the least of which were the 6x6 trucks and Weasels.

Studebaker entered the postwar era in December 1945 with 1946 Champion cars that basically were warmed over 1942's. Studebaker's first new postwar cars introduced in May 1946 were the revolutionary designed 1947's styled by Raymond Loewy, the noted industrial designer. Automotive historians regard the 1947 Studebakers as the first new car design in America since 1941, particularly as Ford, General Motors and Chrysler did not introduce their postwar designs until the 1949 model year. Most cars were manufactured in the South Bend, Indiana plant, although some were built in the Los Angeles, California facility. Studebaker's first convertible since 1938 was marketed in 1947. During the years 1947 through 1954, the Commander was the high priced series while the Champion was the low priced series.

By the 1948 model year, another passenger car manufacturing plant was opened in Canada. During the 1948-1954 period, the company slowly implemented a marketing plan to promote the Land Cruiser, originally the most prestigious Commander, as a separate model if not series. Studebaker's internal records indicate, however, that the Land Cruiser continued to be referenced as part of the Commander line. Starting with the 1949 model year, body style "C", the five passenger coupe, was re-designated the Starlight Coupe. Some automotive historians have applied the Starlight name retroactively to the 1947 and 1948 "C" bodies, although Studebaker did not.

In 1950, the "bullet-nose" front end provided some major design changes to the original 1947 styling. The first Studebakers with automatic transmission were available in 1950. In a record production year, some 320,884 cars were sold. Economy vehicles introduced at mid-year called Champion Customs remained in the product lineup through 1955. Externally, the 1951 cars were very similar to the 1950's, as the vehicles shared the same wheelbase and body shell, except for the Land Cruiser. For Studebaker, 1951 was the V-8 year, with this power plant standard for Land Cruisers and Commanders and optional on Champions.

In the Centennial year of 1952, the cars were face lifted and the "bullet nose" design replaced by more traditional automotive styling. The Korean War created steel shortages which resulted in much lower production than in previous years. Studebaker introduced an all new design by Loewy for 1953, which featured beautiful Starlight and Starliner coupes that won many design awards. Studebaker marketed these new products as the "American car with the European look," but customers did not respond and sales continued to fall. While the 1953 Loewy European look pleased design critics, potential customers appeared to be turned off by the company's lack of self-confidence in America's future by implying that European was better than American.

The highlight of 1954 was the corporate merger of the Studebaker Corporation and the Packard Motor Car Company into Studebaker-Packard, which soon became dominated by former Packard executives. The Studebaker product lineup included a new two-door station wagon named Conestoga because the company marketing geniuses thought that nostalgia would sell, which it didn't. Unfortunately Conestoga looked backward just when Chrysler developed its new line of forward looking cars. Also a first was an ambulance package that converted the Conestoga into an Ambulet. Another special kit allowed commercial owners to convert the station wagons into panel expresses. After a

nine model year absence in the product line, the President was restored as the top of the line series in 1955. The Land Cruiser was replaced by the President State sedan. The unique President Speedster hardtop was introduced in January, 1955 as a special one year model.

The thoughtful redesign that characterized the 1956 models made the cars much more handsome. These models were more American looking, which suggested the abandonment of the Studebaker style since the 1947 cars. The old Starliner and Starlight coupes were redesigned by Loewy into a new series of coupes and hardtops known as the Hawks. Sales fell in 1956 and consequently the Los Angeles manufacturing plant closed permanently.

The 1957's were minimally changed from the 1956's, although four-door station wagons were added to the model lineup. Company officials recognized that in a recession, the buying public might welcome an economy car. A mid-year introduction, the Champion Scotsman, provided dealers with such a car, one year before American Motors offered the 1958 Rambler. The Scotsman, with painted grille and hub caps and without side trim molding, eventually became a separate series although not a best seller and corporate sales continued to decrease. The Scotsman marketing concept again related to an old European legend, this time the thrifty Scot when perhaps a better appeal would have been to emphasize America's continuing interest in high technology, which of course the Scotsman wasn't.

In 1958, Studebaker placed a greater priority on selling such specialty vehicles as four-door Ambulets and Econ-O-Miler taxicabs. But, only 44,759 cars were sold in the last year that Studebaker made standard sized passenger cars. If the company did not make a dramatic and strategic move quickly, Studebaker faced bankruptcy. The introduction of compact cars in 1959 to compete both with American Motors and the Big Three was the Studebaker solution to this problem.

1946 Skyway Champion three-passenger coupe.

1946 Skyway Champion five-passenger club sedan.

1946 Skyway Champion six-passenger cruising sedan.

1946 station wagon with body by Mifflinburg.

1947 Commander Regal De Luxe five-passenger coupe.

1947 Commander Regal De Luxe convertible coupe.

1947 small-scale design model produced under the direction of Raymond Lowey.

1947 Champion De Luxe three-passenger coupe.

1947 Champion De Luxe five-passenger coupe.

1947 Champion Regal De Luxe two-door sedan.

1947 Champion De Luxe six-passenger sedan.

1947 Champion Regal De Luxe four-passenger convertible coupe.

Raymond Loewy's personal 1947 car.

1947 experimental Champion station wagon, designed by Raymond Lowey but not produced.

1948 Champion De Luxe three-passenger coupe.

1948 Champion De Luxe two-door sedan.

1948 Champion Regal De Luxe four-door sedan.

1948 Champion Regal De Luxe five-passenger coupe.

1948 Champion Regal De Luxe convertible coupe.

1948 Commander Regal De Luxe two-door sedan.

1948 Commander Regal De Luxe five-passenger coupe.

1948 Commander
Regal De Luxe
four-door sedan.

1948 Commander Regal De Luxe four-door sedan.

1948 Commander Land Cruiser four-door sedan.

1948 Commander Land Cruiser four-door sedans.

1948 Commander Regal De Luxe five-passenger convertible coupe.

The 1949 final assembly line.

1949 Champion De Luxe three-passenger coupe.

1949 Commander Regal De Luxe two-door sedan.

1949 Champion Regal De Luxe five-passenger Starlight coupe.

1949 Champion Regal De Luxe five-passenger convertible coupe.

1949 station wagon with body by Cantrell.

1949 Commander Land Cruiser six-passenger sedan.

1949 Commander Regal De Luxe convertible coupe.

1950 Champion Regal De Luxe four-door sedan. The millionth post-war vehicle, with Studebaker president Harold S. Vance at the wheel.

1950 Champion Regal De Luxe three-passenger coupe.

1950 Champion Regal De Luxe five-passenger Starlight coupe.

1950 Champion Regal De Luxe two-door sedan.

1950 Champion De Luxe four-door sedan.

1950 Champion Regal De Luxe convertible coupe.

1950 Commander Regal De Luxe two-door sedan.

1950 Commander Regal De Luxe four-door sedan.

1950 Commander Regal De Luxe Starlight five-passenger coupe.

1950 Regal De Luxe Land Cruiser four-door sedan.

1950 Commander Regal convertible coupe and Miss Arizona.

1950 Commander Regal De Luxe convertible coupe.

1950 Commander five-passenger sedan "sand car" developed for Arabian American Oil Company.

1950 station wagon with body by Cantrell.

1951 Champion Custom three-passenger coupe.

1951 Champion Regal three-passenger coupe.

1951 Champion five-passenger coupe.

1951 Champion Custom two-door sedan.

1951 Champion Regal two-door sedan.

1951 Champion Custom Starlight coupe.

1951 Champion Custom four-door sedan.

1951 Champion De Luxe four-door sedan.

1951 Champion Regal Starlight five-passenger coupe.

1951 Commander State Starlight coupe.

1951 Commander State two-door sedan.

1951 Commander State four-door sedan.

1951 Commander Land Cruiser four-door sedan.

1951 Commander convertible coupe.

1951 Commander State convertible coupe.

1952 Champion De Luxe two-door sedan.

1952 Champion Regal four-door sedan.

1952 Champion De Luxe Starlight five-passenger coupe.

1952 Champion Regal Starliner five-passenger hardtop coupe.

1952 Champion Regal convertible coupe.

In 1952 Dwight Eisenhower campaigns in South Bend.

1952 Commander State convertible. *From the collection of Asa E. Hall.*

1952 Commander State Starlight five-passenger hardtop coupe.

1952 Commander Regal two-door sedan.

1952 Commander State four-door sedan.

Prototype 1952 Commander Starliner hardtop coupe, based on a 1951 vehicle.

The 1952 assembly line.

Studebaker president Harold S. Vance inspecting a 1952 Commander State Starliner hardtop coupe.

1953 Champion Regal Starlight five-passenger coupe and Studebaker vice-presidents Elliot and Peterson.

1953 Champion Starliner two-door hardtop.

1953 Champion De Luxe two-door sedan.

1953 Champion Regal four-door sedan.

Studebaker president Harold S. Vance and 1953 Champion Starlight hardtop coupe.

1953 Champion Starliner hardtop two-door coupe.

1953 Commander Starliner hardtop two-door coupe.

1953 Commander De Luxe two-door sedan.

1953 Commander Regal four-door sedan.

1953 Commander Land Cruiser four-door sedan.

1953 Commander Regal Starlight hardtop coupe.

Raymond Lowey with his personal car, the 1953 Special Landau Coupe.

The first 1954 Studebaker delivered to a retail customer.

1954 Champion De Luxe Starlight two-door coupe.

1954 Champion Regal two-door hardtop coupe.

1955 Champion Custom four-door sedan.

1955 Champion De Luxe four-door sedan.

1954 Champion De Luxe four-door sedan.

1954 Champion Conestoga two-door station wagon.

1954 Champion Regal four-door sedan entered in the Mobilgas Economy Run.

1954 Champion Custom four-door taxicab photographed in Manila.

1954 Commander Regal Starlight five-passenger coupe.

1954 Commander De Luxe four-door sedan.

1954 Land Cruiser Regal four-door sedan.

1954 Commander Regal Conestoga two-door station wagon.

1954 Commander De Luxe Conestoga Ambulet.

1954 Commander Regal sedan delivery.

The 1954 Canadian assembly line.

1955 Commander De Luxe two-door coupe.

1955 Commander Regal four-door sedan.

1955 Commander Regal Conestoga two-door station wagon.

1955 Commander Conestoga station wagon.

1955 Commander Conestoga Ambulet.

1955 President State four-door sedan.

1955 President State two-door coupe.

1955 President Speedster hardtop coupe coming off the assembly line.

1955 President Speedster hardtop coupe.

1956 Champion four-door sedan.

1956 Champion Econ-O-Miler taxicab.

Pre-production 1956 Commander four-door sedan.

1956 Commander Marshal four-door sedan.

1956 President four-door sedan.

1956 President Marshal four-door sedan.

1956 President Pinehurst station wagon.

1956 President Sky Hawk two-door hardtop coupe.

1956 Champion Flight Hawk two-door coupe.

1956 Golden Hawk two-door hardtop coupe.

1957 Champion Scotsman two-door station wagon.

1957 Champion De Luxe four-door sedan.

1957 Champion Pelham two-door station wagon.

1957 Commander Parkview two-door station wagon.

1957 Commander Parkview two-door sedan delivery.

1957 President Classic four-door sedan.

1957 President four-door sedan and Parkview Ambulet with Broadmoor emblem.

1957 Silver Hawk five-passenger coupe.

1957 Golden Hawk two-door hardtop coupe.

1958 Champion two-door sedan.

1958 President two-door hardtop coupe.

1958 President four-door sedan.

1958 President Broadmoor four-door station wagon.

1958 Silver Hawk two-door hardtop coupe.

1958 Golden Hawk hardtop coupe.

The photographs reproduced in this book are from the collection of Shelby and Howard Applegate. Many of the photographs, as well as thousands of others of American passenger cars and commercial vehicles, are available at wholesale or retail. Studebaker car and truck original sales literature, owner manuals, tune-up charts, paint charts, and stock certificates also are available, as is similar material on most popular American and foreign marques. Inquiries from buyers and sellers of automobilia are invited.

APPLEGATE AND APPLEGATE
PO BOX 260
ANNVILLE, PENNSYLVANIA 17003

EVENING TELEPHONE: (717) 964-2350

The Iconografix Photo Archive Series includes:

JOHN DEERE MODEL D Photo Archive	ISBN 1-882256-00-X
JOHN DEERE MODEL A Photo Archive	ISBN 1-882256-12-3
JOHN DEERE MODEL B Photo Archive	ISBN 1-882256-01-8
JOHN DEERE 30 SERIES Photo Archive	ISBN 1-882256-13-1
FARMALL REGULAR Photo Archive	ISBN 1-882256-14-X
FARMALL F-SERIES Photo Archive	ISBN 1-882256-02-6
FARMALL MODEL H Photo Archive	ISBN 1-882256-03-4
FARMALL MODEL M Photo Archive	ISBN 1-882256-15-8
CATERPILLAR THIRTY Photo Archive	ISBN 1-882256-04-2
CATERPILLAR SIXTY Photo Archive	ISBN 1-882256-05-0
CATERPILLAR MILITARY TRACTORS VOLUME 1 Photo Archive	ISBN 1-882256-16-6
CATERPILLAR MILITARY TRACTORS VOLUME 2 Photo Archive	ISBN 1-882256-17-4
TWIN CITY TRACTOR Photo Archive	ISBN 1-882256-06-9
MINNEAPOLIS-MOLINE U-SERIES Photo Archive	ISBN 1-882256-07-7
HART-PARR Photo Archive	ISBN 1-882256-08-5
OLIVER TRACTORS Photo Archive	ISBN 1-882256-09-3
HOLT TRACTORS Photo Archive	ISBN 1-882256-10-7
RUSSELL GRADERS Photo Archive	ISBN 1-882256-11-5
MACK MODEL AB Photo Archive	ISBN 1-882256-18-2
MACK MODEL B 1953-66 Photo Archive	ISBN 1-882256-19-0
MACK FC, FCSW & NW1936-1947 Photo Archive	ISBN 1-882256-28-X
MACK EB, EC, ED, EE, EF, EG & DE 1936-1951 Photo Archive	ISBN 1-882256-29-8

LE MANS 1950: THE BRIGGS CUNNINGHAM CAMPAIGN Photo Archive	ISBN 1-882256-21-2
SEBRING 12-HOUR RACE 1970 Photo Archive	ISBN 1-882256-20-4
IMPERIAL 1955-1963 Photo Archive	ISBN 1-882256-22-0
IMPERIAL 1964-1968 Photo Archive	ISBN 1-882256-23-9
STUDEBAKER 1933-1942 Photo Archive	ISBN 1-882256-24-7
STUDEBAKER 1946-1958 Photo Archive	ISBN 1-882256-25-5
AMERICAN SERVICE STATIONS 1935-1943 Photo Archive	ISBN 1-882256-27-1
CASE TRACTORS 1912-1959 Photo Archive	ISBN 1-882256-32-8
FORDSON 1917-1928 Photo Archive	ISBN 1-882256-33-6
Available Late 1995	
MACK MODEL B 1953-1966 VOL.2 Photo Archive	ISBN 1-882256-34-4
MACK FG-FH-FJ-FK-FN-FP-FT-FW 1937-1950 Photo Archive	ISBN 1-882256-35-2
DODGE TRUCKS 1929-1947 Photo Archive	ISBN 1-882256-36-0
DODGE TRUCKS 1948-1961 Photo Archive	ISBN 1-882256-37-9
MACK EH-EJ-EM-EQ-ER-ES 1936-1950 Photo Archive	ISBN 1-882256-39-5
MACK LF-LH-LJ-LM-LT 1940-1956 Photo Archive	ISBN 1-882256-38-7
STUDEBAKER TRUCKS 1928-1940 Photo Archive	ISBN 1-882256-40-9
STUDEBAKER TRUCKS 1941-1964 Photo Archive	ISBN 1-882256-41-7

The Iconografix Photo Archive Series is available from direct mail specialty book dealers and bookstores throughout the world, or can be ordered from the publisher.

For information write to:

Iconografix
PO Box 609
Osceola, Wisconsin 54020 USA

Telephone: (715) 294-2792
(800) 289-3504 (USA and Canada)
Fax: (715) 294-3414